I Love Hate My Hair

(My Journey with Alopecia)

Tamara N. Harvey

Copyright © 2016 by Tamara N. Harvey

All rights reserved.

This book or any portion thereof may not be reproduced or used in any manner whatsoever without the express written permission of the publisher except for the use of brief quotations in a book review.

Printed in the United States of America

First Printing, 2016

ISBN: 978-1-5356-0054-5

Contents

Introduction 1
I'm Losing My Hair (1998) 3
Protective Styling (2002 – 2004) 7
I'm Getting Married (2006) 10
Family First (2007) 12
Back to Work (Summer 2009) 14
Where Are My Brows? (Winter 2014) 18
Something Unique (Christmas 2014) 21
A Message to Stylists 24
My Methods of Treatment 26
How Much Does Hair Loss Cost? 30
Social Media 32
The Person Within 34
When I Look in the Mirror 35

Introduction

OVER 20 MILLION WOMEN IN the United States alone, are suffering from some type of hair loss. This does not take into account the rest of the world, and a little less than half are under 40 years of age. The emotional effects of hair loss range from anxiety and depression, to frustration and poor self-esteem. Fortunately, there are more options available now, to help slow down and even reverse hair loss in women. (Her Alopecia, 2003-2008)

Androgenetic alopecia (AGA) is the most common form of hair loss in women. This type of hereditary hair loss can begin any time after puberty and usually occurs, if at all, before the age of forty. For me it began when I was 28.

Over the past 18 years I have been consumed with what to do about losing my hair. From the thinning, to the very first bald spot, and now the complete loss in my crown. After each stage I just kept asking myself "*So Now What?*"

I was motivated to write this book to share my story and how I have been dealing with AGA; and to provide you with information as well as resources that can help you or someone you know who may have alopecia. It has also been somewhat therapeutic to just release all of the thoughts and experiences. When I used to get down about losing my hair I would read scriptures, motivational quotes; and I have included some of my favorites at the end of each chapter.

I have endured a lot during my journey with alopecia. Although it won't kill me, I am living with this forever! The obstacles that I faced during all my major life changes (marriage, pregnancy) and the numerous stylists I have seen, and methods of treatments I have tried to maintain and regrow my hair. The astronomical amount of money I have spent. And most recently losing my eyebrows.

This book will help you understand what the different types of alopecia are; and some of the suggested tests and treatments that are available. If you are someone who has alopecia, I hope it will encourage you to take the steps to start and hopefully find a solution to your specific situation.

In the beginning, I never found out if there were any specific 'underlying causes' related to my hair loss. I just took the hand I was given and dealt with it the best way I could.

"The only thing harder than dealing with hair loss as a woman is thinking you're the one this is happening to."
~ Women's Hair Loss Project ~

I'm Losing My Hair (1998)

Prior to my hair loss, I used to wear my hair short and sassy and was going to a salon called Short Cutz. Towanda Solese was my stylist at the time, and short styles were her specialty. If you wanted precision and razor cutting then Towanda was your stylist. Although I did not have any noticeable hair loss when I was going to Towanda at Short Cutz, I mention her now because this was my 'favorite' style; and I will see her again later on during my journey. Short styles are very manageable and easy to care for and I used to like to add an extra pop of color to it, such as strawberry blonde. I must say, back in the day—I LOVED MY HAIR!

I was twenty-eight years old when I first realized I was losing my hair. My boyfriend was standing over me and said that he noticed a small bald spot in the center of my head. At first I just thought it was from the constant circular motion from me wearing my hair in a "wrap style," but then as time went on I felt like it might be more. Like, was all the wear and tear on my hair causing the damage? I mean, back then I was straightening my hair with chemical relaxers and would often use temporary or permanent colors as well.

In 2000, I was going to a stylist named Tonya, who worked at a place called Salon Plaza. Tonya would style my hair in roller sets so it would look fuller, put it in up-do styles so the bald spot wouldn't be seen, but to no avail. I was still young and wanted to be adventurous with my hair and wear it in different styles. The up-do styles were okay and the roller sets lasted a little longer, but I still wanted to do more. I never had a problem with my hair growing, but you know the expression – "Your hair is your crowning glory!" But when your hair is primarily falling out in the crown area, a lot of styles are just not doable. So let me tell you that this "thinning" or "bald spot" was not sitting well with me.

Styled by Towanda Solese! Prior to the onset of my hair loss

A few months later, I went to the dermatologist to find out exactly what was going on with my hair and if there was anything that I could do to stop, prevent, or at least slow down the hair loss. During my visit, I had a scalp biopsy and was later told I had Androgenetic alopecia, and that my hair loss was more than likely a result of 1) traction damage (from the different styles I wore my hair in) and also the chemicals, and 2) genetics (male/female-pattern baldness).

For those of you who do not know, Alopecia simply means "hair loss", and there are three different terms that include the word alopecia: • Alopecia Totalis • Alopecia Universalis • Androgenetic Alopecia. The American Hair Loss Association defines the terms as follows:

Alopecia Totalis

Alopecia totalis is thought to be an autoimmune disorder that causes loss of all head hair. Unlike androgenetic alopecia (male- or female- pattern baldness), there are no remaining patches or areas with hair on the scalp once alopecia totalis has run its course. It is still questionably believed that *stress* is a major contributing factor in causing alopecia totalis, despite the fact that many people who suffer from it report low stress levels.

Alopecia Universalis

Also sometimes called alopecia areata universalis, alopecia universalis is the term used to describe rapid loss of hair all over the body. It includes head hair, eyebrows, and even eyelashes. It is the most severe form of hair loss and is believed to be an autoimmune disorder. While many treatments have been explored, no standard treatments exist for this condition.

Androgenetic Alopecia

Androgenetic alopecia is the most common type of hair loss. It is also referred to as male- or female-pattern hair loss and is abbreviated as AGA. Heredity and hormones are the two major factors that can cause this type of hair loss. Androgenetic alopecia causes more than 95% of hair loss in men. Women are greatly affected by it as well, in part due to the same genetic factors found in men as well as other contributing factors like ovarian cysts, high androgen index birth control pills, pregnancy, and menopause. (American Hair Loss Association, n.d.)

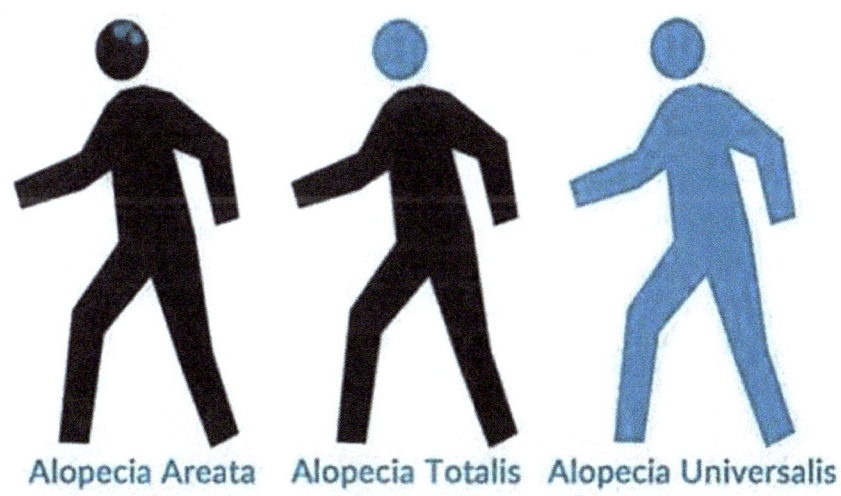

(Different Stages of Alopecia)

Tamara N. Harvey

The Ludwig Scale classification of female pattern baldness
The Ludwig Classification System describes hair loss patterns in female pattern baldness, which ranges from stages I to III. This illustration is a simplified version.

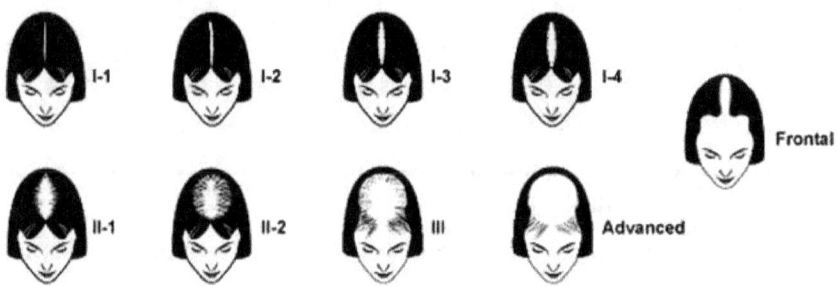

*NOTE: In 1998 I was at Stage I-1 and today I am at the Advanced Stage. (Harris, n.d.)

The dermatologist informed me that Rogaine, a topical treatment containing minoxidil, was the only thing that was proven to stimulate hair growth; however, since I was in my child-bearing years it was not recommended for me to use at the time. So I started using shampoos like NIOXIN for thickening, and went to the health store and stocked up on vitamins for my hair, skin and nails. I stopped going to the Salon Plaza and was referred to another stylist named Maxine Dyett by a friend. At the time Maxine would style my hair in flexi rods and up-dos to hide the bald spot. After a year or two I stopped going to the salon altogether because I feared that relaxing my hair would make it come out faster. I couldn't believe that I was thinking about this and I had just celebrated my thirtieth birthday. *So now what?*

"Do not give up, the beginning is always the hardest."
~ Alopecia Quote ~

Protective Styling (2002 – 2004)

I WAS TOTALLY CONVINCED NOW that I would only wear my hair in protective styles. Which meant my new place to go for styling was the African Braiding House. "Protective styling is any style that conceals the ends of the hair protecting them from damage caused by overexposure to the elements, friction and environmental pollution. Low manipulation styling is any style that requires minimal styling or upkeep.

The key to a protective style is protecting the hair from over-manipulation, chemical and environmental elements. Natural hair is fragile. We have tightly curly hair or coiling hairs that wrap themselves around one another and cause tangles, snaps, and knots.

There needs to be breaks in between protective styles as the hair needs time to breathe as well as rest. Most protective styles add stress to the hair and that is not including the major detangling session you will encounter after the take-down of the style. Deep conditioners and protein conditioners are crucial and will help but there needs to be a break between each stint to give your hair some down-time.

You have to be mindful of too much tension on your hair with protective styling also. Excessive wear and tear on your hairline can weaken it and break it off. This is another reason why breaks in between are necessary along with making sure the style is not too tight or you may take a braid and your own hair off during take-down.

When wearing protective styling your hair needs moisture, natural oils and to be cleansed regularly. Neglect is the quickest way to find dry brittle strands during your take-down so know that you do not get a break from caring for your tresses when they are in a protective style." (When Protective Styling Goes Wrong: Explaining Common Issues, n.d.)

I went to the African Braiding House every three months or so, and sat through hours of various braided styles like singles, micro minis, kinky twists and cornrows. Not putting any chemical relaxers or heat to my hair for over a year was beneficial. Until one day the stylist there told me that she would not do my hair anymore as it was thinning badly and they did not want to hinder it further.

I went back to Towanda, and she took care of my hair for me for about a year. I did go back to a chemical relaxer to wear my hair straight and curled. I used to feel so guilty when I went to the salon because I felt like I was putting so much pressure on my stylists to fix my hair. But Towanda did not mind, in fact, she was very patient and honest with me about what she could or could not do to help me. As we noticed the spot getting larger, I asked her about hair extensions or weaves. Since short cuts were her specialty, at the time she did not style hair using those accessories, so I knew I had to find someone else. If you are in the DC/Maryland/Virginia area and are looking for a "short cut" specialist I strongly recommend Towanda Solese—view her bio on the Salontra Select Suites website at http://www.salontraselectsuites.com/location/catonsville/towanda-solese.

By 2005 I was really in a rut. Unsure of what to do with my hair and who to go to next, I did the next best thing for me—to take care of my hair myself. Which meant going back to the basics and possibly going back natural-depending on how long it would take me to find another stylist. My bald spot was larger now, somewhere in between II-1 and II-2 on the Ludwig Scale, but I still had my hairline, thank goodness. That made it easier to wash and style my hair while still being able to cover up the bald spot. The only thing that made me smile these days was the fact that I was engaged and planning one of the biggest days of my life. *So now what?*

> *"I Love my NATURAL HAIR because it is a gift that we as BLACK WOMEN have."*
> ∼*Lola Atobatele*∼

I'm Getting Married (2006)

I WAS SO SCARED AND anxious about how I would wear my hair on the wedding day. And you know I wanted my hair to be right for that day. With the protective styling my hair grew out very nice so in spite of the bald spot, I had a nice bit of length to it. I went searching online for some places that would help me with my problem. First, I visited the Hair Club®, but didn't like what they had to offer. Then one day I was browsing through one of the local circulars that came to the house and I found this salon called Versacchi. I was like, "Versacchi," huh…okay let me give them a call. LOL.

I visited Versacchi Studios and had a private consultation. After the consultation I was excited and considered purchasing one of their hair enhancers. Although the enhancer would definitely work and correct my problem, I decided not to purchase it because I didn't want to have something that I would have to remove and install myself (even with clips). Especially on my wedding day/night. I wanted something permanent that would just blend in with my real hair. But almost a decade later, I referred a friend to Versacchi Studios and she was elated with the service and quality of her hair enhancer. Visit their website at: http://www.versacchi.com/.

My cousin referred me to a young lady named Pamela Johnson and suggested that I go talk to her. So I did and Pam assured me that she could fix my hair for the wedding and cover my bald spot. Lo and behold, she did, using hair extensions. And on my wedding day I LOVED MY HAIR. The photos were beautiful and I was worry free that day and on the honeymoon. I was so happy with Pam's work that I continued to go to her for styling for the next two years.

I Love/Hate My Hair

September 2007 - Styled by Pamela Johnson of Salon JusJah's!

    I have to take my hat off to Pam because in order to do my hair she had to shampoo, set me under the dryer, add the hair extensions, cut them, and curl my hair. Every two weeks! On top of that, every six to eight weeks I usually got a chemical relaxer. As clients, we complain about the location of the salon, the prices, staffing changes and sometimes the wait, but the stylists are faced with many challenges as well. That's why I always say "you have to have a skill to do hair"—it's truly something special and I am so grateful for ALL of the ladies who have helped me over the years.

    Soon after the wedding, my work schedule changed drastically and I could no longer keep my regular hair appointments. *So now what?*

"Life is an endless struggle full of frustrations and challenges, but eventually you find a hairstylist you like."

∼Author unknown∼

Family First (2007)

My husband and I had talked about starting a family almost immediately after we were married Labor Day Weekend of 2007. By this time I was thirty-seven years old and I felt like my clock was ticking. But, after trying for almost a year, we were expecting-with twins! I can't even explain the joy and excitement we were feeling.

Because of the consistent use of glue to keep the hair extensions in place, my hair loss sped up a bit. All I could think was God I HATE MY HAIR! I don't want to be this ugly pregnant lady with a bald spot. What am I going to do? Pam helped me work through my hair styles while I was in my first and second trimester, but by the third I was put on bed rest and in the hospital for the duration of the pregnancy.

One night while lying in the maternity wing of Greater Baltimore Medical Center (GBMC), I literally took the hospital lotion and loosened my hair extensions right out of my head. And from that point on, I wore a head wrap/scarf. While I was in the hospital I was depressed and did not want any visitors besides my family and close friend. During my stay at GBMC, I was always in my hospital gown or nightgown and would have false contractions and get rushed to another location to make sure the babies were okay. Then one day my mommy came in with a girlfriend.

Not an actual person though; a wig. I call my wigs my girlfriends. LOL. It wasn't anything fancy, just a bob style with a bang. And I wore that wig most of the time while I was in the hospital from November 2008 to January 2009. Those few weeks seemed like they were the longest weeks of my life. By the grace of God I was able to carry them up to thirty-six weeks and delivered a healthy baby boy, Jonathan, and baby girl, Janell.

I Love/Hate My Hair

Me & ALL My Girlfriends over the Years! ☺

Over the next six to nine months I wore my girlfriend faithfully. Between the prenatal vitamins during the pregnancy and wearing it in cornrows, my hair had grown out to shoulder length (except the bald spot smack dab in the middle). Working out at home and caring for the twins while on maternity leave was a task in itself and to not have to worry about my hair was a relief. I didn't have to go out every day for work so I could walk around all day half bald if I wanted to. But as you can guess, I grew tired of the wig and wanted to run my fingers through my own hair again. Plus my six months of maternity leave were almost up. *So now what?*

"I can't tell you what a pleasure it is just to put my hair under a wig cap and slap on a wig that's already done." Its dress up for your hair."
~Felicity Huffman~

Back to Work (Summer 2009)

A COWORKER REFERRED ME TO this young lady named Larnell Lancaster and told me that she worked with cancer patients and also with women and men who just needed help with their hair loss. Larnell offered what she called a "unit," which just covered my bald area. The unit is applied directly to your scalp, and held in place with either bonding glue or tape. After securing, the hair on the unit can be cut, styled and blended with your real hair as desired. I was reluctant at first because I thought, this is a toupee! Well, that is exactly what it was, and it was just right. I went to see Larnell for a consultation and she told me all about the unit and how she could make it blend in with my real hair. She took measurements of my hair loss area and before you knew it I was in her chair having my hair unit installed. Oh how I LOVED MY HAIR! But about a year later, Larnell changed careers and was no longer doing hair full time, so once again I was faced with the horrible idea of who was going to do my hair. *So now what?*

One Saturday morning I took a trip to the local beauty store, Beauty4U, to look at their wigs and to check out the stylists that worked there. While looking at some wigs, I met a young lady named Alithea Robinson (Lisa). Lisa is the owner of Hair Weaves and Extensions and she talked with me about my hair and the possibility of trying out a weave. So in the fall of 2010 I got my first hair weave and I LOVED MY HAIR! You can see me in my first weave on Lisa's website at http://www.hairweavesandextensionsmd.com.

Over the next three to four years I would continue to wear weaves and/or natural styles with partial weaves by Lisa. Her creativity was unbelievable and the work seemed effortless. But after a while I felt like

Easter 2010 – Wearing my first hair unit - Styled by Larnell Lancaster!

wearing the weaves has started to affect my hair loss even more. Eventually the entire front of my hairline was gone, with the exception of a few strands (Ludwig Scale - III). This was a problem for me, but not for Lisa. She still managed to "make it work" by extending the braids across my bald spot and connecting to the hair on the other side. A hair net, some thread and extensions, and voila! Lisa also offers her own products, called 'TRUTH', for her clients to maintain our hairstyles in between visits. I use the Rosemary Tea Tree Oil and Conditioner Pomade for me and my daughter. Out of all the techniques that I have tried, I did like the weaves and partial weaves best. My hair grew nicely while I wore them and they were manageable and easy to care for. I usually would keep them in for up to three months without any problems. Lisa would create custom colors, and use different textures of hair to make each weave unique. So now when I shop for a new girlfriend, I often purchase ones that are similar to a weave style that I have had.

Various styles created by Lisa at Hair weaves and Extensions!

By the end of 2013, I was in between wearing the full weaves and partial weaves and natural braiding styles, and I wanted something different. So I scheduled an appointment with Pam. Why? Because she "slays with the scissors" and I wanted a haircut, but not my real hair. At the time, I was taking the Hairfinity® challenge and I had her cut off all of the chemically relaxed hair that was left and give me a quick glue-in style. (This glue-in style was created by using a REMY Bump kit that you can purchase at the local beauty store, like Beauty4U (http://www.bty4u.com). Most often your real hair is protected with a stocking cap or hairnet so the glue is not applied to your real hair or scalp.) Well, the style was short and sassy, like only Pam could do, and coming into the New Year in 2014 I can truly say that I LOVED MY HAIR! Visit Pam's Facebook page at: https://www.facebook.com/Salonjusjahs.

I Love/Hate My Hair

By the summer of 2014 I had stopped getting weaves and went back to buying different wigs and working on keeping my real hair in the best possible condition that I could. It's tough for me to leave a stylist because I do have "hairdresser loyalty." I know that might sound strange, but once you get comfortable with someone and they can help you with your problem you don't want to let them go. There is the frustration and anxiety when you expose yourself to another new stylist and another salon full of new clients. Plus, I was always hoping that something or someone would help me bring my hair back. – But it never happened! *So now what?*

> *"Your hair is a statement of style, an affirmation*
> *of beauty, and an expression of self-love."*
> *~Ademola Mandella~*

Where Are My Brows? (Winter 2014)

YES, YOU READ RIGHT. NOW my eyebrows are completely gone. Over the past few years I realized that they were thinning—no! Damn near gone!—and I had resorted to drawing them on every morning to the best of my ability. I even purchased some eyebrow templates to help me with filling them in. Until one day I was sweating so bad that I wiped my face and didn't even know that one was gone. That was it. I knew I had to do something. I didn't even bother going back to the dermatologist because I just figured, well, this must be another form of alopecia (alopecia areata), but I was praying I wouldn't lose my lashes, too!

I was curious to find out what could cause 'Eyebrow Loss' so I did a quick Google search and found this information from the Live Strong website. "Eyebrow loss, also known as superciliary madarosis, can occur with a variety of medical conditions. Madarosis can affect one or both eyebrows with partial or complete hair loss. Infections, chronic skin disorders, hormone disturbances, autoimmune diseases, and medications are among many medical reasons for eyebrow loss. In most cases, identification and treatment of the underlying condition leads to regrowth of the eyebrows. Permanent eyebrow loss can occur with disorders that permanently damage the hair follicles. Some of the medical reasons listed for eyebrow loss were:

- Chemotherapy
- Hypothyroidism
- Atopic Dermatitis
- Alopecia Areata
- Hansen's disease

View the website for the specifics on each of the medical reasons. (John, 2015) http://www.livestrong.com

I Love/Hate My Hair

I remembered a friend telling me that his wife got her eyebrows permanently tattooed on, so I went online and searched for places in the DC/Maryland/Virginia area that could help me with cosmetic surgery. I found a place called Permanent Cosmetics in Columbia, Maryland. I called and spoke with the owner, Susan Davis, and scheduled an appointment.

I went alone because I didn't know what to expect and, quite frankly, wasn't sure how I would look. Seeing the before and after pictures in Susan's office gave me confidence that this procedure would definitely be a good investment. I was surprised that it only took about an hour and by how great a job Susan did freehand. By the time I got to her my natural brow line, etc., was gone. She drew them on first with a pencil based on the shape that I told her I liked and the color of my hair. On November

Tamara N. Harvey

25, 2014, I said, "I LOVE MY BROWS!" I would recommend anyone to Susan who wants fuller brows or needs brand-new ones. Visit her website at https://www.permanentcosmeticsofmaryland.com.

"Defined brows instantly make you look more polished."
~Bobbi Brown~

Something Unique (Christmas 2014)

WHENEVER I WANTED A NEW look (girlfriend) I would go to the local beauty store because they were reasonably priced but I wanted to splurge and have one made. I follow a young lady named Quandra Johnson, owner of Unique Hair Experience, on Instagram (@unique_hair). And she would wear and post pictures of herself and clients in these fabulous wigs that she made. Well, I told my mother that I just had to have one. So I communicated with Quandra (Que) and sent her pictures of my hair etc. and she said that instead of giving me a weave she would make something special for me. On December 17, 2014, I walked out of that salon wearing a custom-made wig made from Indian Curly Hair in lengths up to twenty inches and colored beautifully. Needless to say, it was flawless! I LOVED MY HAIR! Visit Que's website at www.uniquehairexperience.com.

I brought in the New Year of 2015 with a new attitude, new hair, and new eyebrows. I was happy. I needed another option to wearing wigs and wanted to have my real hair styled again. So I called one of my stylists from the past, Maxine Dyett, now owner of Max & Co Salon and Hair Loss Center. I spoke to Maxine about my hair-loss situation and went in for a consultation. Since Maxine had not done my hair in a few years, she was not aware of the amount of hair loss I now had (Ludgwig Scale-Advanced). Once she saw me, I don't think she was that shocked, as her experience in the field has shown her more clients than ever who are experiencing hair loss. Maxine had the hair units like Larnell, and since I was familiar with that I went and placed my order for one. It was February 27, 2015, when Maxine fit my unit and cut and styled me the cutest short and sassy hairstyle. I LOVED MY HAIR! Visit Maxine's website at https://www.facebook.com/Max-Co-Salon-and-Hair-Loss-Center-571023216278204/.

December 2014 - Custom Wig made by Quandra Johnson of Unique Hair Experience!

By the end of the year and my forty-sixth birthday pre-menopausal symptoms set in and I could barely get through the workday without breaking into a sweat at the drop of a dime. Oh, and the night sweats. So off came the unit and I was back at the beauty store looking for a new girlfriend. I really didn't want to get another one because the combination of the wig caps and girlfriends really break off my edges. But what was I going to do? And the girlfriends help me to express how I am feeling on any particular day. One day I might wear one that is brown with highlights, short and curly, and the next day I'm dark, straight, and twenty inches. A girl can never have too many options, and that is exactly what girlfriends give me, and it also keeps them guessing.

I Love/Hate My Hair

February 2015, hair unit installed by Maxine Dyett, Max & Co Salon and Hair Loss Center

"Gorgeous Hair is the Best Revenge."
~ Ivana Trump ~

A Message to Stylists

THIS CHAPTER IS BY NO means a backlash toward any of the stylists whom I have been or will be a client of. It is just a gentle message for them to consider their clients' feelings when they are consulting those of us who are suffering from "special" problems with their hair like alopecia.

The majority of the clients in the salon do not have any major hair problems, or at least not like mine. So when I am sitting in the chair, vulnerable and exposed, they look, whisper, and who knows, maybe have even snapped a pic on the sneak. And I am not alone. I have a friend who told me she was left in the middle of the salon wide open for any and everyone to see. Imagine that for a moment. You walk in (more than likely having already told the stylists about your situation) and are taken to the first, second, or third seat in the front of the salon. And you have to take off your wig, head wrap, hat, or whatever you came in with to cover your bald head.

If nothing else, I think the stylists should at least consider taking the client into a private room, if there is one, or in the break room in the back, or someplace where only YOU and HE/SHE can see and discuss your situation. It really makes a difference.

It just so happens that I have come to grips with my hair and how it looks uncovered so I have sat exposed at some salons, but there has been a time or two when I just felt like, this is so not cool! Most of us with alopecia are sensitive about the subject, and all we ask is that you give us some privacy to discuss our problem.

Take the time to educate yourselves about more than just how to style hair, especially with clients with alopecia. It's obvious that this is a real problem for more clients than ever and even some of you. There is no doubt that we depend on each other and the expectations from both are great. To me you all are more than just a stylist, you are a friend. I appreciate your kindness, lending ear, morale boosting, confidence building and self-esteem building talent. Thank You! ☺

When I contacted Towanda to let her know that I was writing this book, she told me about a very informative class she attended called, 'The Truth About Ethnic Hair Loss'. The training was provided by Certified Ethnic Alopeciologist, Cyndie Smith. Cyndie is the Director of Education at the Hair Wellness Institute (HWI).

I told Towanda that I had briefly met Cyndie at Maxine's salon a few months prior. And that I would include this information for any other stylists who may be interested in attending. Visit the HWI website for more information: http://www.hwicourses.com/

> *"I think that the most important thing a woman can have next to talent, of course is her hairdresser."*
> *∼Joan Crawford∼*

My Methods of Treatment

OVER THESE PAST TEN-PLUS YEARS, I feel like I have tried everything. There would be mornings when I sat at my vanity getting ready for work, or nights at bed time and I would just cry. Looking at all of the stuff that I had for my hair. And for what? I still had this huge bald spot. Sometimes I would call my mom or a friend and tell them how I just did not want to do it that day. I would look in the mirror and felt like I didn't want to wear any of my wigs, or I didn't like the way my weave looked after I washed it, or that my hair unit was lifting. I would be so frustrated, and sometimes it would be hard to pull it together. That's when my mom used to say, "Never look how you feel." And those were the days that I wore a nice dress, high heels and my favorite red lipstick.

Other than vitamins that I used from the GNC, and various shampoos for thickening, etc., I really didn't believe that any product would help my hair grow any faster or denser. In 2013, I saw a post on Facebook and Instagram for some hair vitamins called Hairfinity®. Of course I ordered them and tried their regimen of vitamins and shampoo for about three months. I did see new growth around my hairline and I did notice that the texture of my hair was more manageable, and my stylist at the time (Lisa) said it felt stronger than ever. After the three months I went back to the GNC vitamins and continued to manage my hair with a lot of moisturizing products while keeping my daily routine as simple as possible. Visit the GNC website to view their products: http://www.gnc.com/

The one ingredient that I saw more of in Hairfinity® (Hairfinity, 2016) was biotin. Visit the website for more information: http://www.hairfinity.com/ GNC's vitamin had biotin in it as well, but not as many micrograms.

Both vitamins worked for me and I have recommended them to my family and friends to try. Just remember: as with most supplements, it is good practice to drink a lot of water while taking them. Another piece of advice would be to use as little heat on your hair as possible. Wearing protective styles really helped me to achieve this.

Now I am trying an oil called Wild Growth® (Wild Growth, 2014) that I saw on Facebook. They offer a three-step Hair Promotion System that includes shampoo, sealing, and texture transformation. I only purchased the one in the white bottle and I only use it in step 3. I have noticed some growth; and my hair is very manageable as it has been months since I have had a relaxer. So most of the new growth I have is in its natural state. Nevertheless, I will finish this bottle of hair oil. Visit the website for more information: http://www.wildgrowthcompany.com/.

Recently I became an It Works!® distributor and plan to use our Hair Skin Nails nourishing complex in the future, and encourage others to do the same. You can purchase them from It Works!® as my Loyal Customer for three months and share your hair growth testimony with me! In 2016 I am on the road to financial freedom and committed to helping others 'Look Younger and Live Longer'. Visit my website at http://tamaraharveywraps.myitworks.com/.

I am back to wearing wigs most days until I decide whether to go back to Maxine and wear Sassy (my hair unit) again. My regular routine of hair care consists of shampooing and conditioning using Mane 'n Tail products. Yup, and I use them on my daughter's hair as well. Funny, one day I purchased some from the beauty store and the clerk asked, "Don't you feel weird using products that are used for animals too?" My response was simply, "Nope!" It works for me and my daughter so I will continue to use it. Of course I give us both hot oil treatments regularly and keep our scalps and hair moisturized with their Moisture Enriched Crème and/or Hair Dressing. I had someone ask me, "Why do you worry about having alopecia so much? It's not going to kill you." My response was simple- "It may not kill me, but I have to deal with it for a lifetime." I had no idea that from that first bald spot I would be where I am today.

Some days I want to go and put the hair unit back on, especially during the spring and summer seasons. But unfortunately, I have to take a break from it because the adhesions (glue/tape) were irritating my scalp. Simple cornrows are working for me under my wigs and at night I sleep with a satin bonnet on my head.

My advice for anyone who has any one or more of the three types of alopecia (areata, totalis, universalis) would be to first seek help from a professional to determine which specific type you have, and then decide what course of action you want to take in maintaining what hair you have left in the healthiest condition possible. Whether that be to cut it all off or wear hair extensions and wigs. Whatever you decide, wear it well!

The Her Alopecia website recommends having the following blood tests and blood work done to diagnose the underlying cause of women's hair Loss:

- DHEA, DHEA Sulfate, Prolactin, Follicle Stimulating (FSH) and Leutinizing Hormone (LH)
- Androstenedione
- Free and Total Testosterone
- Thyroid Tests: T-3, T-4, and Thyroid Stimulating Hormone (TSH)
- Iron and Serium Ferritin and Total Iron Binding Capacity (TIBC)
- Hemoglobin/Hematocrit or CBC (Complete Blood Count)

Discuss with your doctor which tests are covered by insurance, and if you've got the means, don't take no for answer. (Her Alopecia, 2003-2008) I did not have any of these tests when I was first diagnosed with alopecia; however, over the years I have had all of them except the Androstenedione and Free and Total Testosterone. My results proved that I do not have an overactive or underactive thyroid; however, my Iron and Ferritin counts were low and I do have a Vitamin D deficiency. Per my Primary Physician, I currently take supplements to increase my levels. I drink a lot of water, get as much rest as possible, and try to maintain my stress level. The dermatologist told me that with the male/female-patterned baldness, there's really nothing you can do about it. I know that genetics played a large part in my hair loss, but I often blame myself for all the damage that I had done to my hair. I also believe now that over the years other contributing factors for me have been ovarian cysts, years of taking birth control pills, my pregnancy and recently perimenopause.

I have included a few pictures from each of the awesome, multi-talented, and creative stylists whose client I have had the privilege of being over the years. I have tried as many hairstyles as products over the years. As you can see, they are very different in styles and textures, and that is what I think makes me unique and special. I used to think about what people would think or say when within a month they saw me go from a short pixie wig to a sixteen- to eighteen-inch weave, but you know, at the end of the day all that matters is what I think and what I see.

"Why fit in when you were born to stand out?"
~Dr. Seuss~

How Much Does Hair Loss Cost?

LET ME BE THE FIRST to tell you "it isn't cheap!" One day I sat down and thought about how much money I may have possibly spent and it just blew my mind. At one point I even considered getting a cosmetology license to educate myself and learn the basics so I can do my own hair and help others with my problem. But I honestly believe you have to have the skills for that and I do not. I will keep my day job, thank you very much.

To try to wrap my head around how much I have spent over the past decade I've used the average price for these basic services: $35 Shampoo/Style + $10 for a cut, and every 6–8 weeks $60–75 (depending which stylist I was going to) = $1500 per year x 10 years= $15,000. The two years I went to the braiding salon with an average style costing anywhere from $100–250 (depending on the style/technique) = $2,500 x 2 years=$5,000. The cost for just the hair extensions or tracks for 2 years: approximately $20/pack every 2 weeks X 2 years = $500.

The first unit that I purchased was approximately $350. The second unit I purchased, in 2015, was $700. I have purchased approximately 10 wigs from the local beauty store, with those prices ranging from $79–175 = $1,000; and my unique wig was $700 including hair, color, and closure. Hair weaves for 4 years averaging from $200–250 at least 4 times a year = $3,600. Permanent Cosmetics for my eyebrows = $575. A grand total of $27,425! Guess we could just round it up to $30,000 for any miscellaneous appointments and/or services.

In my case I know it's a lot more than that, but for the sake of my alopecia journey I am just counting from 1998 to the present. I have been going to the hair salon since I was in middle school, when my hair was burned out with the straightening comb and I had to go and get a Jheri curl to bring it back to life. Wonder whatever happened to those? LOL.

No doubt the hair industry is prosperous. Especially the black hair care industry. I mean, everywhere you look you see our faces and images promoting all things hair. The Huffington Post reported that market-research firm Mintel estimated the size of the 2012 market at $684 million, with a projection of $761 million by 2017. But Mintel also notes:

What's missing from these figures are general market brands, weaves, extensions, wigs, independent beauty supply stores, distributors, e-commerce, styling tools and appliances. If all of those things were to be taken into consideration, the $684 million in expenditures could reach a whopping half trillion dollars. Half trillion, as in $500 billion. (Opiah, 2014)

~*"Invest in Your Hair – You Wear it Every Day"*~

Social Media

I BELIEVE THAT A LOT of the pressure women feel about their looks comes from what society perceives as acceptable and beautiful. Celebrities are almost always picture perfect and often trend setters with their hair and clothing. We see them in Hollywood, on television, in movies, and in concert effortlessly wearing clothes from the best fashion designers; and gracing the covers of magazines looking flawless. Today, social media is usually the first place people go to emulate these looks.

In an effort to keep up with them, individuals join social media sites to follow their favorite celebrities. The most popular internet and reality television stars have over 40 million followers. This gives them a lot of power and influence over what people see and how they think. It may also have a huge impact on our self-esteem. The first thing Users check on most of their social media sites is what is trending. The Top 20 trending topics on Twitter is discussed everywhere by everyone. At work, in magazine articles, by radio station hosts, and the evening news sometimes will report on them. Just put a hashtag in front of a word and there you have it. You can start a movement that will go on forever.

The most important thing for individuals to remember about social media is that although your favorite actor, singer, writer, or friend does or says something, it is ultimately you who has to make the right and final decision. Constantly looking at those 'picture perfect' posts can reduce your self-esteem and ultimately lead you to have feelings of low self-worth. I recommend everyone take a break from social media at least once – even if it's just for a week.

I joined Facebook in 2009 when my twins were born. Initially to communicate with family and friends and post pictures to capture the memories of our twins growing up and events we attend, etc. Today I still post cute pictures of the kids and I love a #Selfie every now and again, but now I find myself using social media to advertise my business or to search for information.

With respect to alopecia, social media provides an abundance of information. For individuals (children and adults) who are living with alopecia, there is information and articles on what symptoms to look for, diagnosis and treatments; and how to support the campaign to find a cure for it. One in particular is the National Alopecia Areata Foundation. Log in to Facebook and search for them-then Like and Follow!

When I joined Instagram a few years later, I saw even more information and awesome posts showing hair stylists who create styles and wigs for men and women who suffer hair loss. These are just a few of my favorite Alopecia related Instagram accounts that I follow:

@alopeciasupport
@aaawareness
@thebaldiemovement
@alopeciaapparel
@hairdoctorfl
@razorchicofatlanta

You can also follow me on Instagram at either my personal account @tamnicharv OR @harvey5911 for my #ILoveHateMyHair Booster T-shirt campaign OR @tamaraharveywraps for my It Works!® account.

"My hair doesn't need to be "Fixed". Society's narrow minded view of "Beauty" is what's Broken."
~ Trichotillomania on Pinterest ~

The Person Within

For man looketh on the outward appearance,
but the Lord looketh on the heart.
– 1 Samuel 16:7

PART OF MY DAILY ROUTINE is to read a passage from a book titled, 'Prayers & Promises for Women'- I felt that this passage from the chapter titled "BEAUTY" was suitable for my book.

(Sorter, Prayers & Promises for Women, 2003)

We are too conscious of outward beauty today, Lord. Our singers, our heroes, our role models – even our politicians – are expected to meet certain standards of beauty. Even worse, we instinctively trust the beautiful, never looking beyond their bodies, as though perfect hair indicates a perfect brain or a pure heart. When we stop to think about it, we know this is foolish, but we rarely do think about it. Make me more conscious of this error, Lord. Teach me to look through appearance when I choose my heroes or my husband. A perfect hairdo should not unduly influence me – it may be warming a very small brain. An expensive Italian suit may very well be covering a dark heart. Help me see beyond beauty- or the lack of it.

When I Look in the Mirror

When I look in the mirror I can still see that little girl leaning over the kitchen sink getting her hair washed, or sitting between her mothers' legs getting her hair parted and plaited. As long as I can remember my hair was always 'done' meaning in a style nice and neat. Edges brushed down smooth and pony tails or plaits secured with barrettes.

When I look in the mirror, I remember how excited I was when I got old enough to have my hair pressed with the straightening comb (hot right off the stove) or after I got my first perm I started using the curling iron; and could roll it up with sponge rollers. That teenager who decided what style she would wear because she was paying for it.

Today, when I look in the mirror I see a beautiful woman who has been beaten down by the thought and reality of losing her hair. The idea that her hair actually makes up who she is. A WOMAN who was once embarrassed and ashamed in her own home of who she really was underneath the wig and the oils, and the pills and the stigma. A woman who didn't want her own husband or children to see her without her girlfriend on, afraid they would laugh or say the wrong thing.

But then I looked in the mirror and said to myself, "You are beautiful with or without HAIR, and your family deserves to see YOU for who YOU REALLY ARE." So off came the wig and the hairnet and I let my children see my bald scalp. I let them feel it and I told them that I had alopecia and that was why I was wearing the wig and extensions. Of course they laughed, because they are children and what else would I expect. But they also felt empathy for me because they could see that it was a sensitive issue for me.

Now my daughter goes with me to help me pick out a new girlfriend and my son hints that I need a new one. My husband says he loves me just the way I am and that no matter what I decide he will support me. Even if I decide to shave it all off, although he won't be the one doing the cutting.

When I look in the mirror I see a woman who hopes that by telling my story, some woman or man will take a stand in their struggle with alopecia and make the best of it. Use the resources that are available to us and improve on your looks the best way that you can. Utilize these multitalented stylists in and around our city to help you and them. I am proud now of what I see in the mirror because, believe it or not, I once was not.

"It's not the load that breaks you down, it's the way you carry it."
~Lena Horne~

End

Works Cited

2014. <http://www.wildgrowthcompany.com>.

2016. <http://www.hairfinity.com>.

American Hair Loss Association. n.d. <http://blog.americanhairloss.org>.

Harris, James. *Hair Sciences Center of Colorado.* n.d. <http://www.hairsciencescenter.com/female-pattern-baldness/>.

Her Alopecia. 2003-2008. <http://www.heralopecia.com>.

John, Dr. Tina M. St. *Medical Reasons for Eyebrow Loss Live Strong.* 15 April 2015. <http://www.livestrong.com>.

Opiah, Antonia. *HuffPost.* 24 January 2014. <http://www.huffpost.com>.

Sorter, Toni. "Prayers & Promises for Women." Sorter, Toni. *Prayers & Promises for Women.* Uhrichsville: Barbour Books, 2003. 22.

When Protective Styling Goes Wrong: Explaining Common Issues. n.d. <http://www.clutchmagonline.com>.

www.ingramcontent.com/pod-product-compliance
Lightning Source LLC
Chambersburg PA
CBHW050047080526
44586CB00014B/1499